TEACHER'S BAG OF TRICKS

101 Instant Lessons for Classroom Fun!

by Patty Nelson

Incentive Publications, Inc.
Nashville, Tennessee

Acknowledgements

To the kids of Sedona, for their enthusiasm toward my ideas and for the fun, memorable days we spent together in the classroom.

Cover and illustrations by Susan Eaddy
Edited by Jennifer R. Goodman

ISBN 0-86530-132-8

Table of Contents

Preface

You've finished your lesson and there's still ten minutes left. It's raining and your plans for outdoor play are foiled. Your class finished their assignment early. What can you do?

Why, pull out your "Bag of Tricks," of course! This wide assortment of art activities, word games, puzzles, brain teasers, and calendar ideas is sure to yield a solution to your problem. There are 101 ideas, ready to fill in those "what-will-I-do-now?" moments during math, science, reading, spelling, writing or art. Each activity is self-contained, requiring no special equipment or elaborate, hard to assemble materials. Many are also suitable for use as introductory motivation or to reinforce and extend a lesson or unit of study. These high-interest activities will help you involve your students in meaningful learning projects with a minimum amount of pre-planning.

Don't get caught in an unplanned moment! Just pull out your "Bag of Tricks" and enchant your students with these exciting activities. Both you and your students will be glad you did!

LEARN A NEW WORD | 1

To help students learn a new word or a hard word, get a mini-magnifying box at a teacher's supply store. Write the hard word on a piece of paper, put the written word in the magnifying box and let the student keep it on his desk. Throughout the day have the student look at the word, say it to himself and by the end of the day the new or hard word has been mastered by the student. It's an easy idea and it makes learning fun.

SANTA STUMPERS | 2

Answer these questions to find out what Santa does not like to find in chimneys on Christmas Eve.

1. What letter is in fat but not in sat?   (f)
2. What letter is in sit but not in set?   (i)
3. What letter is in red but not in bed?   (r)
4. What letter is in tree but not in try?   (e)
5. What letter is in sew but not in new?   (s)

Answer these questions to find out what Santa has on his sleigh.

1. What letter is in ball but not in all?   (b)
2. What letter is in set but not in sit?   (e)
3. What letter is in owl but not in owe?   (l)
4. What letter is in owls but not in owes?   (l)

3 | CATEGORIES

The teacher (or leader of the game) thinks of a category and names some words that fit into that category. The class listens to the words named, tries to figure out how the words are related, and then names the category.

Example: Category: Things that are soft.
Words named for the class - sponge, baby's skin, chamois, fur, etc.

Other possible categories to use:

1. Things that are hot
2. Things that melt
3. Non-living things
4. Names of tools
5. Whole numbers
6. Even numbers
7. Fractions

8. Names of fruits
9. Names of vegetables
10. Odd numbers
11. Things made of paper
12. Names of authors
13. Boys' names
14. Kinds of trees

Write the letters of the alphabet vertically on the left side of a piece of paper. Then on the right side write the alphabet vertically again, starting with z and writing it backwards. The object of the game is to see who can make the most words starting with the letter in the left column and ending with the letter in the right column.

Example: A   Z
         B   Y
         C   X
         etc.

Other variations of this game can be to use names of students in your class, spelling words, vocabulary, etc. Have fun! It's challenging!

Read these sentences to your students and see if they can find the state hidden in each sentence.

1. Did you see Ida hoeing the potatoes?   (Idaho)
2. I saw Sam washing tonight at the lake.   (Washington)
3. John will color a doe in the picture.   (Colorado)
4. Neva, darling, how are you today?   (Nevada)
5. While playing Monopoly, he put a
   house on Park Place.   (Utah)
6. Did Ore go now?   (Oregon)
7. Who has seen Tex as an actor?   (Texas)

IDAHO

See if you can name the correct letters. Example: 2 letters that name a girl or boy's name. (KC)

2 letters that mean "to rot."	(DK)
2 letters that mean "jealous."	(NV)
3 letters that mean "the opposite of friend."	(NME)
2 letters that mean "the opposite of not enough."	(XS)
3 letters that mean "extreme happiness."	(XTC)

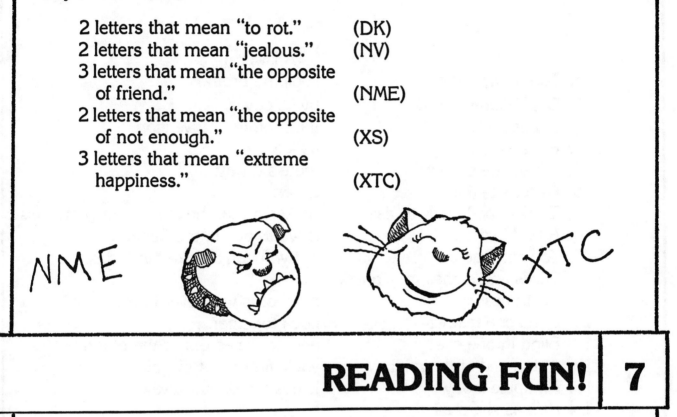

NME   XTC

Put the following teaser on the board and ask the students to try reading it. It is not as easy as it looks! Give the students ample time to try to figure it out.

1 1 was a race horse	(One-one was a racehorse.
2 2 was 1 2	Two-two was one, too.
1 1 1 1 race	One-one won one race.
2 2 1 1 2	Two-two won one, too!)
1 8 0	(I ate nothing!)
1 0 0	(I owe nothing!)
He 8 0 4 A .	(He ate nothing for a period.)

8 | FAMOUS SAYINGS

Listed below are famous sayings. Read them to your students and see if they can finish each one.

(Answers)

1. Too many cooks — spoil the broth.
2. Don't judge a book — by its cover.
3. Necessity is — the mother of invention.
4. He is as cold — as ice.
5. Where there's a will — there's a way.
6. Better late than — never.
7. Early to bed, early to rise — makes a man healthy, wealthy and wise.
8. A bird in the hand — is worth two in the bush.
9. You can lead a horse to water — but you can't make him drink.
10. Sticks and stones may break my bones — but words will never hurt me.
11. Birds of a feather — flock together.
12. Blind in one eye — and can't see out of the other.
13. At the end of the rainbow — you'll find a pot of gold.
14. An apple a day — keeps the doctor away.
15. He's as sharp as — a tack.
16. A penny saved — is a penny earned.
17. Honesty is — the best policy.
18. He's as honest — as the day is long.
19. I wouldn't touch that — with a ten-foot pole.
20. Good as — gold.
21. Happy as — a lark.
22. Feed a cold, — starve a fever.
23. Fighting like — cats and dogs.
24. He's treading on — thin ice.
25. Haste makes — waste.

BUILD A SENTENCE STORY! | 9

Have the students write a story by building onto the first sentence. If, for example, the theme is animals, have the students write about an animal of their choice and then cut out the pages and the cover in the shape of that animal. Have each sentence begin on a separate page.

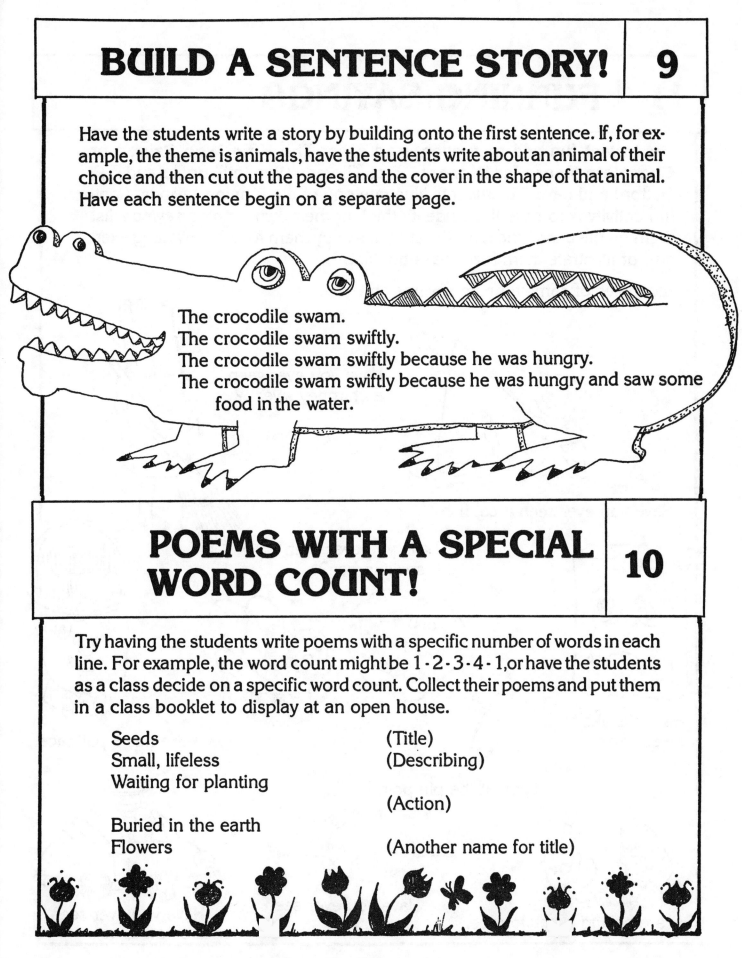

The crocodile swam.
The crocodile swam swiftly.
The crocodile swam swiftly because he was hungry.
The crocodile swam swiftly because he was hungry and saw some food in the water.

POEMS WITH A SPECIAL WORD COUNT! | 10

Try having the students write poems with a specific number of words in each line. For example, the word count might be 1 - 2 - 3 - 4 - 1, or have the students as a class decide on a specific word count. Collect their poems and put them in a class booklet to display at an open house.

Seeds	(Title)
Small, lifeless	(Describing)
Waiting for planting	
	(Action)
Buried in the earth	
Flowers	(Another name for title)

For instant fun and motivation, read either **The King Who Rained** or **Chocolate Moose for Dinner** by Fred Gwynne (Windmill Books and E.P. Dutton) and have the students illustrate one of the funning sayings. Another fun activity is to have the students think of their own funning sayings, list them on the board and have the students copy them for a handwriting exercise or illustrate them for a class booklet.

Examples of some funning sayings are:

Have you ever seen a chimney sweep?

Have you ever seen a cat fish?

Have you ever seen a spelling bee?

He looks like a sad sack.

He has a pail face.

Look at the pin point!

They are having a potato race.

Have you ever seen an egg roll?

Have you ever seen a screw driver?

Ask the students to write picture poems. Provide several examples to help get them in the mood. After they have written their picture poems, have them color and illustrate the paper to make a class booklet.

Examples:

Cinquains are poems made up of five lines with a syllable count of 2·4·6·8·2. The subjects are unlimited. After giving the students several examples, have them write their own cinquains. Then, let them illustrate the poems and make a class booklet.

Droplets
Blue, wet water
Falling, softly downward
Giving moisture to the flowers
Rain drops

Have fun with homonyms! Homonyms are words that sound alike but have different meanings. See if you can find the nineteen pairs of homonyms in the word search below.

ANSWERS:

		two/to
eight/ate	berry/bury	creek/creak
wholly/holy	night/knight	beat/beet
cents/sense	bee/be	red/read
pale/pail	ant/aunt	need/knead
feet/feat	board/bored	aloud/allowed
meat/meet	pair/pear	close/clothes

Have fun with anagrams! An anagram is a word that is made by rearranging the letters of another word.

Have the students think of an anagram for each of the following words. Encouage them to create some anagram posters of their own to hang in the classroom.

bat	(tab)
ape	(pea)
stop	(post)
flea	(leaf)
gum	(mug)
owl	(low)
nat	(tan)
grin	(ring)
melon	(lemon)
tone	(note)
rope	(pore)
tap	(pat)

Below are some examples of anagram posters.

blowing   bowling   top   pot

This fun language arts activity takes only minutes to prepare and the only materials you need are paper and pencils. You will need an 8½" x 11" sheet of white paper for each student in the class. Prepare this lesson ahead of time by making a squiggle on each piece of paper. During language arts time, give each student a piece of paper with a squiggle. The student is to make a drawing using the squiggle as the main focus of the illustration. After completing the illustration, have the student write a sentence, paragraph or story about his squiggle. (The degree of difficulty will be determined by the grade level.) This activity provides the students with a chance for fun and creativity.

Below are some examples that you might want to share with the class.

Have each student in the class draw a monster. Tell the student not to make it too detailed. Then divide the class into pairs. Have the paired students sit back to back so that partners cannot see their drawing. Using only one-way communication, have one student communicate to the other student how to draw his monster. When this monster has been drawn, compare the monster picture to the original drawing to see how well the students communicated to each other. Then, reverse roles. After each student has had a chance to draw a monster, share the pictures with the class and discuss possible ways of communicating better.

The students can also draw animals, flowers, etc.

18 DRAW GEOMETRIC SHAPES IN A SPECIFIC PATTERN

Give each student in the class a piece of paper and a pencil. The teacher may give the one-way communication directions or one of the students may do so. Remember, the drawers cannot ask questions. Have the children draw the shapes in the exact placement as they are drawn below.

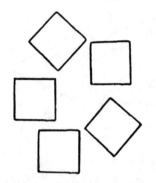

Try other shapes in other positions. Divide the class into pairs to try more new ideas.

19 USING PUZZLE PIECES TO FORM A "T"

Have one student act as the communicator. Have that student stand in front of the room with his back to the rest of the class. The communicator, using one-way communication, is to tell the class how to put the "T" together. Remember no questions are to be asked. This is fun, challenging and very hard to do. Several students might want to try to be the communicator before the solution to the "T" is given.

Solution:

Have the class cut out the pieces below for the "T" one-way communication activity.

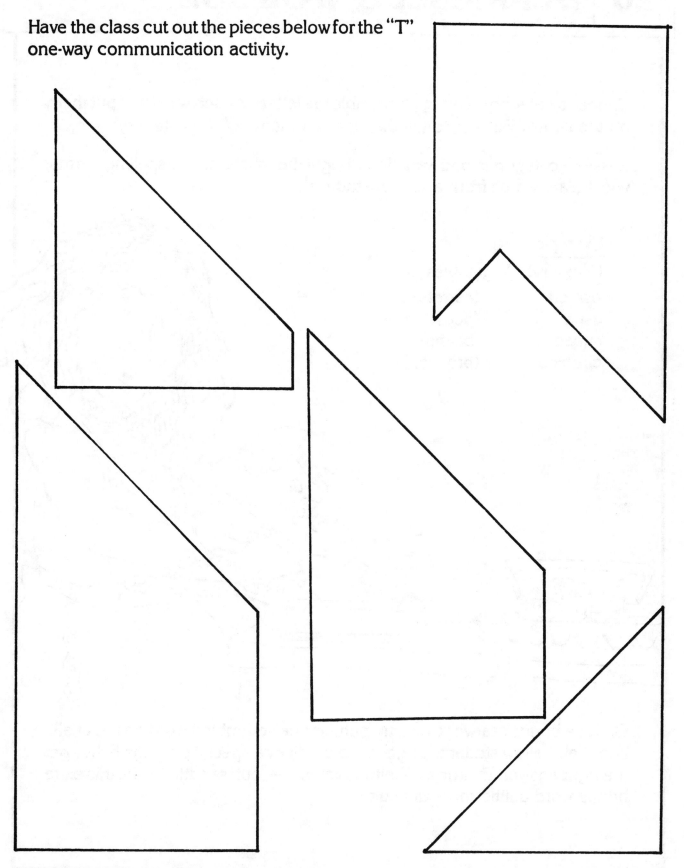

Choose a category of words. Scramble the letters in each word and put them on the board. Be sure to tell the class the name of the category.

Possible categories and variations might be: fruits, tools, spelling words, vocabulary words from a unit of study, etc.

<u>Example</u>

Category: Vegetables

osracrt   (carrots)
aspe   (peas)
snbae   (beans)
ciroblco   (broccoli)

Or, for a bonus seatwork idea, try putting one scrambled word on the chalkboard and allow students to get extra credit or a special privilege if they get the right answer. Example: "United States" — ieutssendtta. Make this extra bonus word a little more difficult.

Make a list of words that have two or three letters in common. Then write a clue for each word on the list Give the clues to students and ask them to figure out the words.

Example: Words that have "UP" in them

Clue	Word	Answer
A baby dog	—up——	(puppy)
Another word for dinner	—up———	(supper)
A student	—up——	(pupil)

Words that have "BOO" in them

A part of a train	——boo——	(caboose)
A pamphlet	boo————	(booklet)
Cowboys wear these	boo——	(boots)

UP	BOO	NO	BY	NO	BOO	UP

FILL IN THE BLANKS | 22

Give the students the initial and final letters of some four letter words and see how many words they can come up with in a specific time.

Example: M __ __ T   (meet, meat, mitt, etc)
          R __ __ D   (road, reed, read, etc)

Another variation would be to give the middle letters and have the students see how many words they can come up with in a specific time.

Example: __ E A __   (meat, beat, seat, etc)
          __ A I __   (rain, pain, raid, etc)

TEAM	MEAT	BEAT	SEAT	NEAT	LEAF

23 | TREASURE BOX SPELLING BEE

you can paint an old lunch pail.

Write all of the spelling words on small slips of paper and put them in a box marked "Treasure Box," or better yet, put them in a box that looks like a "Treasure Box." Divide the class into teams and have each student, in turn come to the treasure box, draw out a word, and spell it.

24 | A WORD WITHIN A WORD

Make a list of words which have smaller words in them. Then take each word on the list and write a clue as to the smaller word within the word. Have a contest with a time limit and see who can find the most words first.

For added variation, have the students make up their own list of words within a word and a clue for each. Trade papers or do them orally at the board. Students love the challenge of thinking of their own ideas, and they love to present them for the class to solve.

Crayon - a streak of sunlight

Newspaper - a place to exercise

supermarket - this makes your hair curly

Example:

Word	Clue		Smaller Word
Stable	A piece of furniture	— — — — —	(table)
Drag	An old piece of cloth	— — —	(rag)
Policeman	Small bugs	— — — —	(lice)

26

Write a word on the chalkboard and have the students see how many different words they can make using only the letters in that word. Each word made from the larger word must be a "real" word.

Examples of some larger words to use:

Disneyland
Pleasure
Challenge
Excitement
Fortunate
Airplane

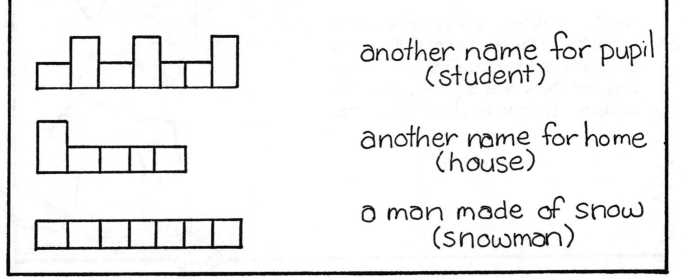

Disneyland
land
snail
day
yield
sidney
is
and
lead
send
dye
die
yes
dale

Have the students take their list of spelling words and make either a crossword puzzle or just a puzzle out of the word and the definitions of the spelling words.

Example:

another name for pupil (student)

another name for home (house)

a man made of snow (snowman)

At a given signal the teacher calls out one letter in the alphabet and the students write as many words as they can think of beginning with that letter. When the teacher calls "stop" all students must put their pencils down. The person with the most "real" words is the winner.

the letter Q

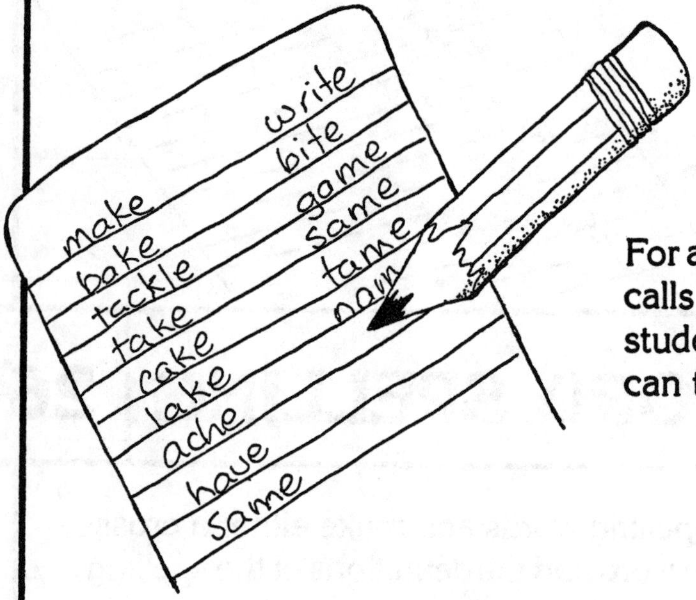

make   write
bake   bite
tackle   game
take   same
cake   tame
lake   name
ache
have
same

For a variation of this game, the teacher calls out one letter in the alphabet and students write as many words as they can think of that end with that letter

I WON!

queen quote
quiz quail
quotient
query quick
quick quill
quarter
aunt quarter
quack

Another variation of this same game might be for the teacher or caller to tell the students to write as many words as they can think of at a given signal that contain a short vowel, long vowel, etc.

To make handwriting more fun try some of these motivators. This is also a good lesson in "following directions."

Tell the students that the follow-up for handwriting will be "handwriting art." The teacher does the drawing step by step on the board while the students use the back of their handwriting paper or a piece of scratch paper. The students are to follow along with the teacher and do exactly what the teacher does on the board. Start the drawing with the letter.

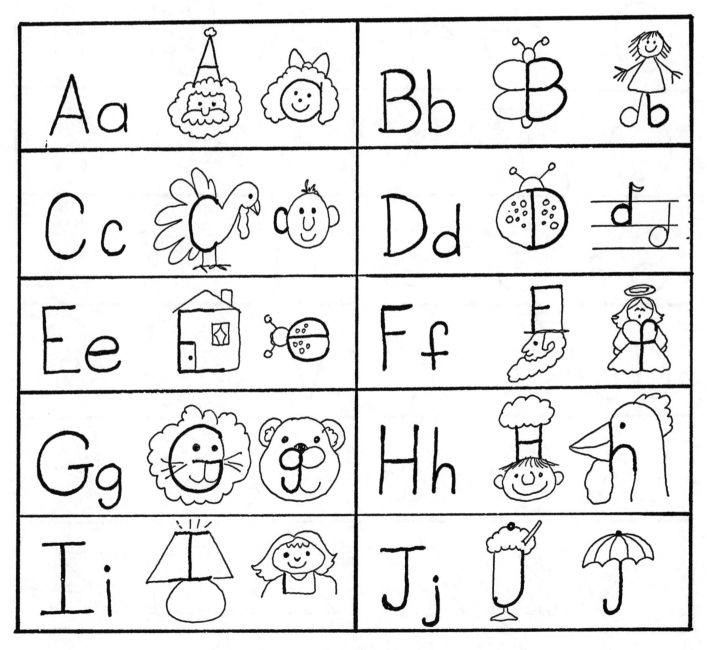

For added fun, have the students draw their own pictures using the letter or letters of the alphabet that you have studied in handwriting that day. Make class booklets out of each letter or have a booklet for each student to draw in during spare time or during "handwriting art."

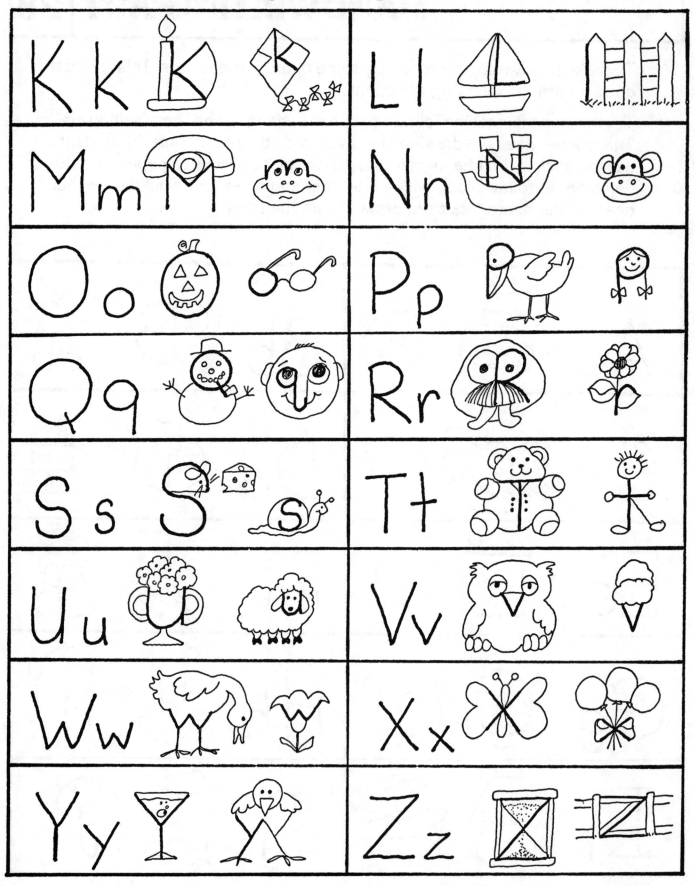

LISTS-LISTS-LISTS | 29

Ask students to sharpen their creative thinking skills by making mind stretching lists. Reading and discussing each other's lists will be almost as stimulating as making the lists. Some lists to begin with might be:

1. A dozen ways to use empty paper cups.
2. A dozen different kinds of fruit used to make jam.
3. Twenty large cities that would be good vacation destinations for kids.
4. Twenty parts of an automobile.
5. Fourteen things kids can do to make money.
6. Ten holidays and one symbol for each.
7. One vegetable (or fruit) beginning with each letter of the alphabet.
8. Twelve foods that come from countries other than your own.

IMPORTANT EVENTS | 30

To help you know more about your students and what they consider important, set aside a block of time for them to write about themselves. Ask each student to select just one thing about their classroom, school or teacher that they feel is important and would not want to give up. Tell the students they may write a story, slogan, paragraph, cartoon, brochure or any other creative writing form they choose, to convey their message. Display the unsigned projects on the bulletin board. It will be fun for students to go to the board in their free time to try to determine the author of each piece. This is a good way for teachers and students to find out what different members of the class value.

31 | LETTERS TO THE AUTHOR

Ask students to select a favorite book and write a letter to the author. Instruct them to tell the author what they liked or disliked about the book, how they would have changed it, what they think of the characters and any other points they consider important. This is a welcome alternative to the tired book report.

Dear Ms. Travers
I Love your Mary Poppins books, I read them over + over. I'm a Wednesday's child like Jane. That sure is a scary story. Maybe it shouldn't be so scary. Jane is my favorite character. I like her because she's spunky. Michael is like my little brother. I wish Mary Poppins lived with me.
Your friend,
Susan ☺

32 | NEWSPAPER DESCRIPTIONS

Ask students to select one item in the classroom that is clearly visible to all. Then pass out copies of old newspapers or magazines. The object of the game is for students to find 20 words to describe the object so that classmates can guess what it is. The words should be cut out and pasted on a sheet of paper. At the end of a given time, students exchange papers and try to identify the object described on the paper they received.

Never throw away a catalog. Ask parents and friends to save theirs for you, too. Then test your creative potential to see how many ways you can think of to use them in your classroom. Here are two for starters.

Catalog Cut-Outs

Pass out catalogs and ask the students to work in small groups to see which group can most quickly find, cut out and paste on a sheet of paper, one of the following:
1. 10 things that go in a box.
2. 10 things that are worn on your head.
3. 10 things that are worn on a cold day.
4. 10 things that use electricity.
5. 10 things that can be used by a pet.
6. 10 things that make work around the house easier.
7. 10 things that kids would like to play with.
8. 10 things that could be taken on a picnic.
9. 10 things that come in pairs.
10. 10 things that cost less than $10.00.

Order Please

Provide a catalog for each student. Specify an amount of money ($50, $60, $100) that may be spent on gifts for each member of the family. Ask the student to fill out the actual order form and stay within the budget. This provides consumer experience in selecting products from a catalog, in filling out an order form and in using math skills. An additional bonus for the activity is the reinforcement of awareness of family member preferences and needs.

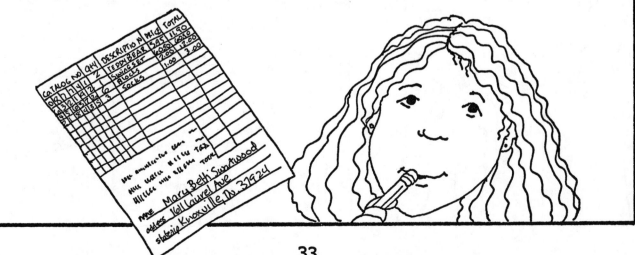

Tell the students that you can tell them how many brothers, sisters and living grandparents they have, if they give you the result of the following steps: (have the students work the steps on a piece of scratch paper)

1. Write down the number of brothers that you have.
2. Multiply that number by 2.
3. Add 3.
4. Multiply that figure by 5.
5. Add the number of sisters that you have.
6. Multiply that figure by 10.
7. Add the number of living grandparents you have.
8. Now tell me your answer.

SOLUTION: Secretly subtract 150 from their answer. The first digit will tell you how many brothers that person has, the second digit will tell how many sisters and the third digit will tell you how many living grandparents

Draw the face below on the chalkboard and have the students look for the numbers 1 to 10. Then have the students make up a Mrs. Number and hide the numbers from 1 to 10 in her face. Have students trade papers and search for the numbers in their classmates' work.

AGE MAGIC | 36

Tell the students that you can tell them their ages if they give you the result of the following steps: (have the students work the steps on a piece of scratch paper)

1. Write down your age.
2. Multiply your age by 3.
3. Add one to the total.
4. Multiply that figure by 3.
5. Add your age to the total.
6. Now tell me your answer.

SOLUTION: Secretly drop the last digit of the answer that they give you and the number remaining will be their age.

$$\cdot \cdot 10 \times 3 = 30 \cdot 30 + 1 = 31 \cdot 31 \times 3 = 93 \cdot 93 + 10 = 103 \cdot \cdot$$

Below are some equations that contain initials of words that will make them correct. Find the missing words.

Example: 12 = M in a Y   ---   12 = months in a year

7 = D in a W	(7 = days in a week)
50 = S in the U.S.	(50 = states in the United States)
12 = N in a D	(12 = number in a dozen)
36 = I in a Y	(36 = inches in a yard)
12 = I in a F	(12 = inches in a foot)
2,000 = P in a T	(2,000 = pounds in a ton)
52 = C in a D	(52 = cards in a deck)
16 = O in a P	(16 = ounces in a pound)
9 = P in the S.S.	(9 = planets in the Solar System)
5 = F on a H	(5 = fingers on a hand)
5 = T on a F	(5 = toes on a foot)
24 = H in a D	(24 = hours in a day)
60 = M in an H	(60 = minutes in an hour)
60 = S in a M	(60 = seconds in a minute)
9 = P on a B.T.	(9 = players on a baseball team)

For added fun have your students make up some of their own equations. Put them on the board and assign them for seatwork or brainstorm them together as a class.

32 = K in our C
32 = kids in our class

57 = D left in S
57 = days left in school

Three men stopped at a hotel for the night. The room was $30 so each man gave the hotel manager $10. After the men went to their room the hotel manager decided that he had over-charged the men by $5. He gave the bell-boy $5 to return to the men. The bellboy decided that it would be too hard to split the $5 three ways so he kept $2 for himself and gave each of the three men $1. That meant that each man paid $9 for the room. $9 × 3 = 27 plus the $2 that the bell-boy kept. WHAT HAPPENED TO THE OTHER $1?

(Answer - Each man paid $8.33 to make $25.00. $25.00 + $3.00 equals $28.00. $28.00 + $2.00 makes $30.00.)

Draw this grid on the chalkboard with the numbers in the squares. Give the students one minute to study the grid with the numbers and then have them duplicate it from memory. How well did they do?

Discuss methods that the students used to help them memorize the grid.

7	24	2	4
1	14	16	6
3	5	21	8

$963 \div 3 = $ __321__

$4 + 6 + 8 = $ __18__

$29 - 3 = $ __26__

$6 \times 11 = $ __66__

$200 + 31 = $ __231__

$37 + 15 = $ __52__

$8 \times 7 = $ __56__

$85 \div 5 = $ __17__

$70 - 20 = $ __50__

$3 \times 6 = $ __18__

$25 \times 6 = $ __150__

$485 + 527 = $ __1,012__

$2,984 + 6,371 = $ __9,355__

0	7	2	1	3	5	4	2	6
8	5	9	4	5	2	1	8	3
2	3	0	7	6	4	5	2	0
5	4	9	8	3	1	7	6	2
3	2	1	9	4	8	7	1	0
0	5	6	3	7	1	5	0	2
1	0	8	5	9	4	3	0	5
4	2	3	5	1	0	1	2	8
8	3	7	2	4	6	5	7	6
6	1	5	4	2	3	1	2	0
2	8	1	7	5	3	6	4	1
4	9	7	5	3	6	8	6	3
3	5	8	8	7	1	4	0	7
6	2	0	2	4	9	2	9	8

Draw the four stars below on the chalkboard. Be sure to label each star exactly as it is labeled in the diagram. (ex. Star #1, Star #2, etc.) Also be sure to write all of the numbers inside the points of the stars exactly as they are given.

Then ask a student to choose one of the numbers written inside one of the points of the stars. Tell him not to tell you what the number is but to tell you which stars the number appears in. (ex. Star #1, Star #2, etc.) Then tell the student that you know (even though he hasn't told you) which number he has chosen. Challenge the rest of the class to figure out how you have done it.

Example: The student chooses the number 6. He tells you that his number appears in Star #1, Star #2 and Star #3. You can figure out the number he has chosen by adding together the numbers of the stars in which the number appears. In this case, you would add together 1+2+3 and get 6 which is the number that the student chose.

Draw the following square on the chalkboard with the letters in their appropriate places. Have the students do this as a group activity and write the number words found on the chalkboard or have them copy the square on a piece of scratch paper. Give them a time limit and see which child can find the most number words. Directions for finding the words:

R	Y	R	V	F
I	T	W	O	I
H	E	N	E	V
R	E	I	S	L
U	O	F	X	R

1. You can go up, down, left, right or diagonally.

2. You are not allowed to skip squares.

3. How many number words can you find?

43 | Egg Carton Math!

This is a fun and simple way to give kids extra practice in addition or multiplication. You will need one egg carton, 3 large lima beans and one felt tip pen. Number the egg carton as shown below using the felt tip pen. Provide the players with 3 lima beans. Each player must place the beans in the carton, close the lid, shake the carton and then add or multiply the three numbers on the spaces where the beans have landed. One point is given each time a player adds or multiplies correctly. The person with the most points at the end of a predetermined number of rounds or time limit is the winner.

44 | Find-A-Number

On 5 x 7 index cards, write activities such as the following:
- Find a number that equals 9 x 7 - 5
- Find a number that is between 359 and 463 and is closer to 473 than it is to 359
- Find a number that is the sum of 17 + 17 + 17 + 19
- Find a number that is close to but less than 972-69

On corresponding index cards, write an answer for each of the Find-A-Number activities.

Place the activity cards in one envelope and the answer cards in another. Students may then use the cards as an individual free time activity or as a game.

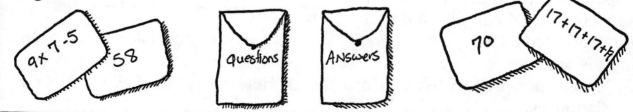

Tired of word search puzzles? Help your students sharpen their math skills with math search puzzles instead. Here's one to get started with.

Find and circle 5 addition equations.
Find and circle 5 subtraction equations.

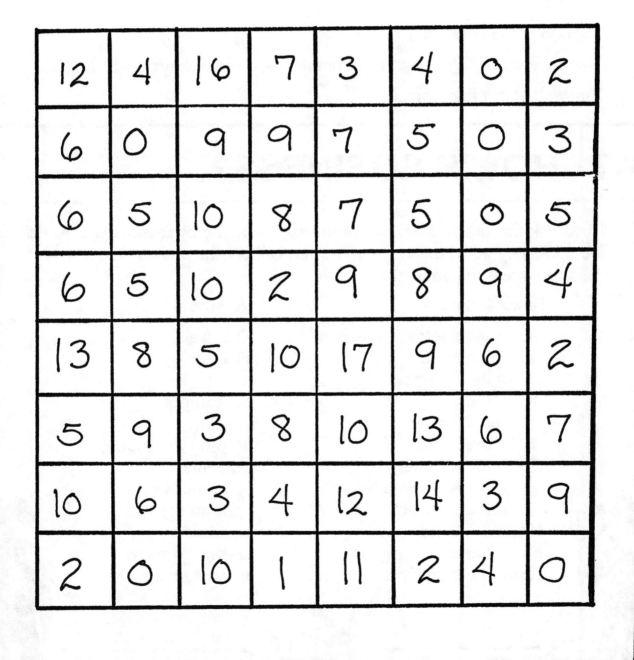

12	4	16	7	3	4	0	2
6	0	9	9	7	5	0	3
6	5	10	8	7	5	0	5
6	5	10	2	9	8	9	4
13	8	5	10	17	9	6	2
5	9	3	8	10	13	6	7
10	6	3	4	12	14	3	9
2	0	10	1	11	2	4	0

46 | RIDDLES

What occurs *once* in every minute, *twice* in every moment but *never* in a thousand years?

(Answer: the letter "m")

What occurs *four* times in every week, *two* times in every month and *once* in a year?

(Answer: the letter "e")

When life gets tough, what is something you can always count on?

(Answer: your fingers)

47 | HOW'S BUSINESS?

If you ask the question "How's business?" to some professionals, how do you think they would answer? Or you can call out the answers & see if your class can guess the professions.

How's business	(Answers)
1. to the doctor	all is well
2. to the author	all write
3. to the milkman	sour
4. to the cook	not too hot
5. to the farmer	growing
6. to the banker	right on the money
7. to the minister	heavenly
8. to the elevator operator	up and down
9. to the architect	right on the line
10. to the tailor	sew-sew
11. to the dentist	having no pains
12. to the laundryman	all washed up

42

These ideas produce instant fun without any preparation on the part of the teacher. All you need is an eager class, chalkboard and chalk.

Read the directions for each pattern and draw the pattern on the board. Let the class provide the solution! Have fun!

See if you can reverse the following pattern of X's in only three moves.

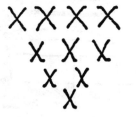

Solution:

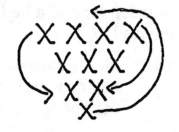

Without lifting your pencil or retracing any of your lines see if you can trace over this entire figure.

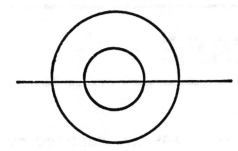

Solution:

Now, try tracing this diagram without lifting your pencil or retracing.

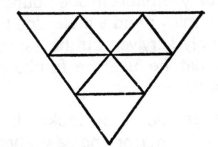

Solution:

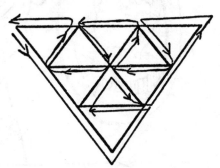

Connect the nine happy faces by drawing only four lines and without lifting your pencil off the paper.

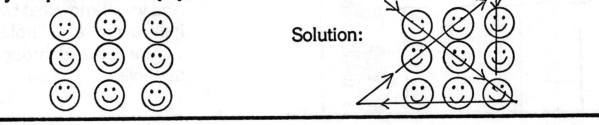

Solution:

49 | HOW DOES HE SURVIVE?

Joe Brown was captured by a group of men and put in a dungeon for a crime that he did not commit. All that was in the dungeon with him was a calendar and a bed. How did he survive?

(Answer: He ate the dates from the calendar and drank from the springs of the bed!)

50 | THE GREAT ESCAPE

Joe Blow was also captured by a group of men and put in a dungeon for a crime that he did not commit. The only furniture in Joe's dungeon was a mirror and a table. Joe Blow not only survived but he escaped! How did he use the furniture to escape?

(Answer: Joe Blow looked in the mirror and saw what he saw. He took the saw and sawed the tabled in half. And we all know that two halves make a "hole" . . . he escaped through the hole!)

Joe Black was also captured by a group of men and put into a dungeon for a crime that he did not commit. The only thing that was in the dungeon with him was a bat. Joe Black not only survived but he, too, escaped! How did he use the bat to get out?

(Answer: Joe Black had the bat in his hands. We all know that in the game of baseball it is "3 strikes and you're OUT!)

CAN YOU SOLVE THESE ABBREVIATIONS? | 52

Write these abbreviations on the chalkboard and see how many the students can solve. Do this activity as a total group, in teams, or individually.

1. pkg.	(package)
2. Dr.	(doctor)
3. Mr.	(mister)
4. govt.	(government)
5. rd.	(road)
6. lbs.	(pounds)
7. inc.	(incorporated)
8. ave.	(avenue)

·govt.· ·lbs.· ·rd.· ·pkg.· ·Dr.· ·inc.· ·ave·

Have the children write down or give orally at least three trivia facts about themselves. Read the lists to the class. Make up a set of trivia questions, pass them out and see how many students can fill in the correct information. For fun, have the students work in pairs or teams.

Example:

1. Who in our class has the most sisters?
2. Which boy in our class was born on Valentine's Day?

A variation of this game might be for the teacher to make up trivia questions about the school.

Mr. Crownoveropteris

Example:

1. How many classes are in our school?
2. What is the name of the teacher with the longest last name?
3. How many different recesses does our school have?

Other fun things to do with trivia in the classroom might be the following:

1. Have several copies of the *Guinness Book of World Records* or *The World Almanac and Book of Facts* and each day on the chalkboard write one to five questions that can be found in either of these books for the students to research. Then sometime during the day these interesting trivia facts can be discussed.

How long is the longest hair in the world?

2. Another idea would be to write some trivia on the board for the students to copy for handwriting. Or, have them copy the answers to the questions written on the board in a notebook to keep for their own fun and entertainment.

Make learning to follow directions fun by asking students to read a "treasure map." The map should have no pictures or illustrations so that students are forced to read the words.

Hint: Have the students do this hunt one at a time. The only preparation you need to do is write the map and leave the bag of goodies (or whatever) with the nurse. Kids love this!

Example:

1. Go out of our classroom.
2. Walk to the swings and pick up one of the pebbles under the swings.

3. Now walk past the principal's office and into the nurse's office.
4. Tell the nurse you are on a treasure hunt and would like the paper bag she has for you.

5. Reach inside the paper bag and take just "one" thing. Give the bag back to the nurse.
6. Come back to the room.

This exercise is fun with all ages! Ask your students these questions about Mother Goose rhymes. When they give an answer, ask them to recite the entire rhyme. This activity is fun and brings back a lot of memories.

Who went up the hill?	Jack & Jill
Who lost her sheep?	Little Bo Peep
Who could eat no lean?	Jack Sprat's wife
Who ran away when the boys came out to play?	Georgie Porgie
Who sat on a wall?	Humpty Dumpty
Who was under the haystack fast asleep?	Little Boy Blue
Whose cupboard was bare?	Old Mother Hubbard
Who had a wife and couldn't keep her?	Peter Peter Pumpkin Eater
Who called for his pipe, bowl & fiddlers?	Old King Cole
Who lived in a shoe?	An Old Woman
Who was frightened by a spider?	Little Miss Muffet
Who jumped over the moon?	The cow
Who ran up the clock?	The mouse
Who kissed the girls and made them cry?	Georgie Porgie
Who was in the Counting House counting his money?	The King
What time was it when the mouse fell down in Hickory Dickory Dock?	1 o'clock
Who is the father of the boy who ate a pie in a corner?	Mr. Horner
Who jumped over a candlestick?	Jack
How many men were in a tub?	Three
What ran away with the spoon?	The dish
Who could eat no fat?	Jack Sprat
Who couldn't put Humpty together again?	All the King's horses and all the King's men
Who was in the parlor eating bread & honey?	The Queen

Use these word pictures for motivators before lessons or for filling in those extra unplanned minutes with fun activities. Put these wordles on the chalkboard one at a time to solve as a group or put ten or more on the chalkboard for the students to solve individually when they finish their work. Have fun!

1.	IDEA	HAIR	DON'T H O R S E	DUOLEBS	T O W N		REACH
2.	CALM	STAND I	WATER	CHAIR	CYCLE CYCLE CYCLE	B A C K
3.	RED	—PROGRAM	TOUCH	SIT IT	SEARCH AND	OFF OFF
4.	FACE	GOING GOING	TENNIS	WEAR LONG	KCUTS	CHICKEN
5.	STAR	(smile)	NEED FRIEND NEED	SIDE SIDE	CRY MILK	B A E DUMR
6.	1	O O CIRCUS O	A CHANCE N	LE VEL	ECNALG	you JUST ME

ANSWERS:
1. Right idea, Haircut, Don't horse around, Mixed doubles, Downtown, Reach out
2. Calm down, I understand, Falling water, Highchair, Tricycle, Back to back
3. Red Cross, Space program, Touchdown, Sit on it, Search high and low, Offsides
4. Face to face, Going around in circles, Tennis elbow, Long underwear, Stuck up, Chicken Little
5. Falling star, Big mouth, Friend in need, Side by side, Cry over spilt milk, Bermuda triangle
6. Hole in one, Three ring circus, An outside chance, Split level, Backward glance, Just between you and me

1.					
BEATING BUSH X (BEATING)	ICE	PRO MISE	HAND (HAND)	R O A D S E K A M → ROADS	iiiiiii O O
2. R|E|A|D|I|N|G	CROSS CROSS	C A L M	(HOLE) ONE	(see above)	PITCH
3. PETE PETE	E T A L B	HEAD HEELS (heart)	HEART	EZ IIIII	MAN / BOARD
4. SYMPHON	BLACK / COAT	LATE / NEVER	GI / CCCCC	DRIBBLE DRIBBLE	F I E L D
5. KNEE LIGHTS	BAR BAR	pineapple cake (upside down)	I'M you	BANANA (vertical)	BAD BAD
6. BALL	THAT THAT THAT THAT	MIND / MATTER	HE AD AC HE	IL TA 'SW	GROUND / FEET FEET / FEET FEET / FEET FEET
7. Strokes STROKES Strokes	FLYING	UP/DOWN 1	YL>#	DICE DICE	(hopscotch) scotch

ANSWERS:
1. Beating around the bush, Thin ice, Broken promise, Hand in hand, Crossroads, Circles under the eyes
2. Reading between the lines, Double cross, Calm down, Hole in one, Makeup, Low pitch
3. Repeat, Round table, Head over heels in love, Heartbreak, Easy on the eyes, Man overboard
4. Unfinished symphony, Black overcoat, Better late than never, G I overseas, Double dribble, Left field
5. Neon lights, Parallel bar, Pineapple upside down cake, I'm bigger than you, Banana split, Too bad
6. Low ball, That's right, Mind over matter, Splitting headache, It's against the law, Six feet underground
7. Different strokes, Flying high, Up one side and down the other, Sidewalk, Paradise, Hopscotch

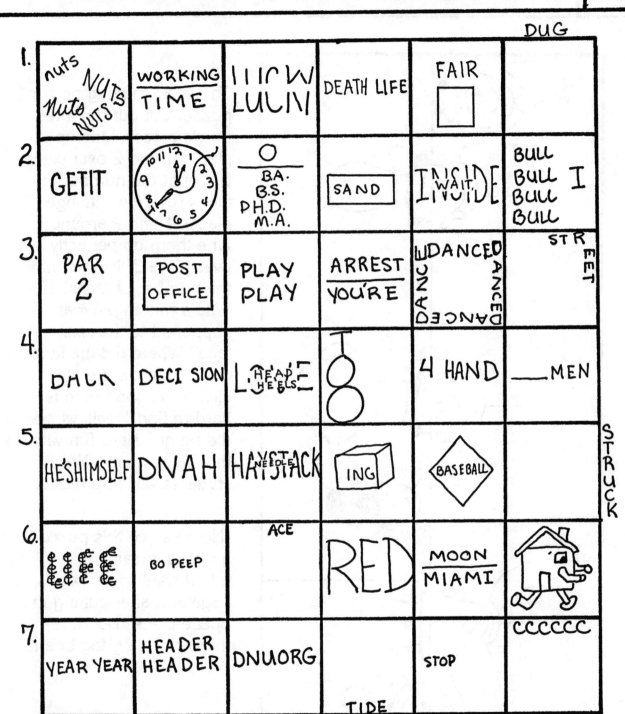

ANSWERS:
1. Mixed nuts, Working overtime, Lucky break, Life after death, Fair and square, Dugout
2. Get with it, Stitch in time, Four degrees below zero, Sandbox, Wait inside, Bull's-eye.
3. Two under par, Post office box, Double play, You're under arrest, Square dancing, Street corner
4. Halfback, Split decision, Head over heels in love, Too big, Forehand, Space men
5. He's by himself, Backhand, Needle in a Haystack, Boxing, Baseball diamond, Struck out
6. Life of ease, Little Bo Peep, Ace high, Big Red, Moon over Miami, Homerun
7. Year after year, Double-header, Background, Low tide, Shortstop, High seas

51

This is a "missing person" puzzle. Cut out the three puzzle pieces. Line up pieces 1 and 2 over piece 3. Count the number of faces (6). Now, change pieces 1 and 2 around. Line them up perfectly over piece 3. Now, count the number of faces? (5) Who's missing? What happened to the sixth face? Where did the face go? You know the old cliche, "A good man is hard to find," well, where did he go? Have fun with this brain teaser. The students will be amazed.

(Note · since this puzzle is a very popular one you might want to xerox this page and after cutting the puzzle pieces out glue them on heavy tag board.)

This is a "missing line" puzzle. Cut out the rectangle and then cut the solid diagonal line in the rectangle. (do not cut the lines with the waves) Hold the two triangles together forming a rectangle. Have the class count the number of lines with waves going through them. (9) Now slide the angle up one line and recount the lines with waves. (8) What happened to the ninth line?

(Note - since this puzzle is very popular you might want to xerox this page and after cutting the 2 puzzle pieces out glue them on heavy tag board)

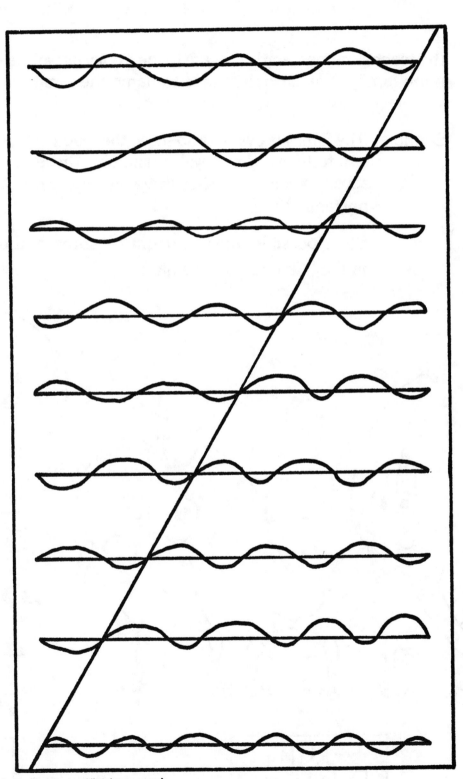

The teacher names words that are in the family as well as words that are not in the family. The class then tries to name the family.

Example: The family is even numbers so the teacher says, "In my family are ten, forty two, four, twelve, and six. These are not in my family: seven, ninety nine, sixty three, twenty seven. Can anyone name my family?"

Other possible families might be some of the ones mentioned in the "Category" word game.

FRUIT FAMILY

ODD NUMBER FAMILY

Most inventions were invented because someone had a problem that needed to be solved. See if your students can solve these problems by matching the inventor to the invention.

INVENTOR	INVENTION	
1. Alexander Graham Bell	The first American Flag	(7)
2. Elias Howe	The electric light bulb	(4)
3. Benjamin Franklin	Products from peanuts	(6)
4. Thomas Edison	The telephone	(1)
5. Eli Whitney	The sewing machine	(2)
6. George Washington Carver	The cotton gin	(5)
7. Betsy Ross	"The Star-Spangled Banner"	(8)
8. Francis Scott Key	The rocking chair	(3)

We all know the saying, "Behind every good man there is a good woman." See how many Presidents of the United States you can match correctly with their wives.

1.	George Washington	Abigail	(4)
2.	Dwight D. Eisenhower	Rosalynn	(5)
3.	Gerald Ford	Mary	(7)
4.	John Adams	Lady Bird	(11)
5.	Jimmy Carter	Bess	(10)
6.	Richard Nixon	Martha	(1)
7.	Abraham Lincoln	Jackie	(12)
8.	James Madison	Mamie	(2)
9.	Ronald Reagan	Dolly	(8)
10.	Harry Truman	Betty	(3)
11.	Lyndon B. Johnson	Nancy	(9)
12.	John F. Kennedy	Pat	(6)

Try this exercise to see how many of your students can recall these famous people and their accomplishments.

1. Maria Tallchief	Founder of Red Cross	(3)
2. Harriet Tubman	Popular singer	(5)
3. Clara Barton	TV star	(6)
4. Bruce Jenner	Treasurer of U.S.	(8)
5. Michael Jackson	Royalty in London	(11)
6. Johnny Carson	An Olympic gold-medal winner	(4)
7. James Monroe	Helped Slaves escape through	
8. Ivy Baker Priest	the underground railroad	(2)
9. Walter Cronkite	A President of the U.S.	(7)
10. Paul Revere	A prima ballerina	(1)
11. Queen Elizabeth	TV news reporter	(9)
12. The Wright Brothers	Famous for his midnight ride	(10)
	First to fly an airplane	(12)

65 | ENTER THE GAME IF YOU CAN!

Here is a fun game. The teacher starts it by naming a word. (frog, for example) Then she names another word which ends with the last letter of frog or whatever word has been named. She continues naming words that begin with the last letter of the previous word until a student catches on. As soon as a student thinks he understands the game, he can name the next word. If the word named is correct have him name two more words to make sure he understands the rule. Then the teacher and the student can take turns naming words until another student catches on to the rule.

Other variations of this game can be:
1. Words that have a long vowel sound.
2. Words that have a short vowel sound.
3. Words that have a double consonant.
4. Words that have two vowels walking. (rain, learn, etc.)

Try creating pictures with words. The possibilities are endless.

TALL SHAKY small
FAT THIN
FALLING CURLY

STAND UP AND TAKE NOTICE! | 67

This is a fun activity that catches the attention of the students and holds it! Write one to five words on the board and tell the students that sometime during the morning (or day) you will be using these words during class. Whenever they hear one of the words being used by the teacher they are to stand. The first person to stand wins a privilege or prize that has been named earlier.

This activity has been used with grades one through eight and the eighth graders seemed to enjoy it the most. The magic words selected can be vocabulary words or interesting words to develop vocabulary. Have fun!

How good is your "Visual Memory"? Try this exercise orally with the entire class.

1. On a stop light, which light is the yellow one - the top, middle or bottom?
2. How many numbers are there in a zip code?
3. Which way does a record turn on a record player - clockwise or counter-clockwise?
4. On which side does the on/off switch appear on an electric typewriter - the left or the right?
5. On which side of the brake is the clutch in a car with manual transmission - the right or the left?
6. On a standard faucet which side is cold - left or right?
7. On a Big Mac do you get one or two meat patties?
8. When a car has two license plates which plate gets the yearly sticker on it?
9. The Statue of Liberty holds her torch in which hand?
10. On which side of the United States is the Atlantic Ocean - the East or the West?
11. On which finger is the wedding ring worn?
12. How many people are on a jury?
13. How many letters are in the English alphabet?
14. Whose face is on a penny?
15. What hand signal does an umpire of a baseball game use to indicate "safe"?

For added fun have the students write some of their own and share them with the class.

ANSWERS: 1. middle, 2. five, 3. clockwise, 4. right, 5. left, 6. right, 7. two, 8. rear, 9. right, 10. East, 11. 3rd finger, left hand, 12. twelve, 13. 26, 14. Abe Lincoln, 15. crosses hands and arms horizontal to the ground

ALPHABETICAL ORDER | 69

Use the successive letters of the alphabet as a determinate for creating a list of words having to do with any given subject. Two or more players may take turns, and the first player not able to come up with an answer loses.

Theme: Animals

Examples: A - Aard-vark
B - Bear
C - Cat

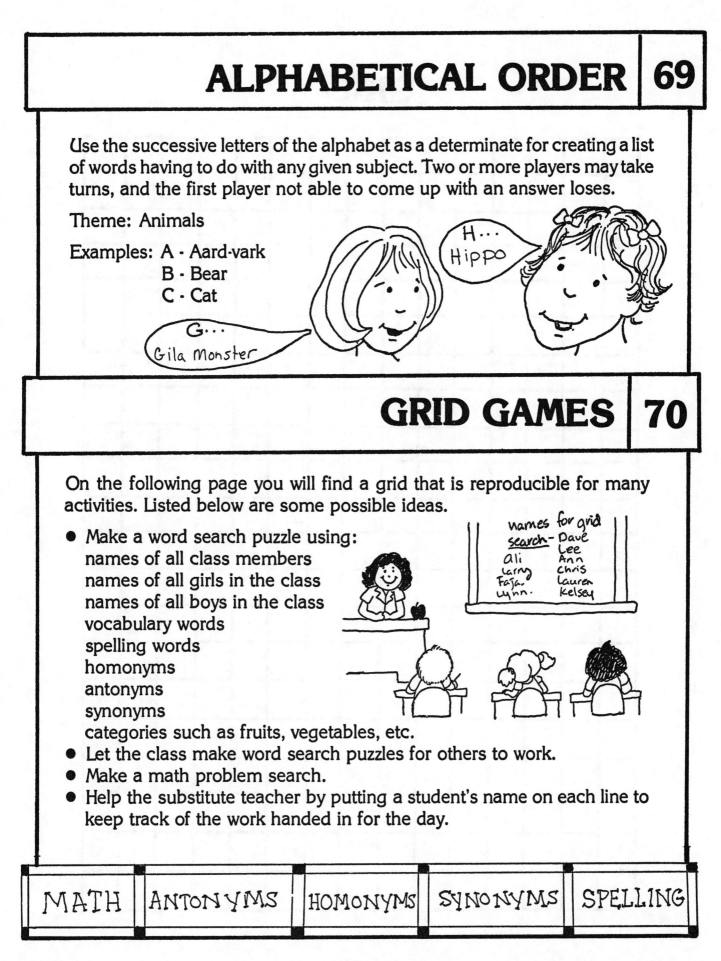

GRID GAMES | 70

On the following page you will find a grid that is reproducible for many activities. Listed below are some possible ideas.

- Make a word search puzzle using:
  names of all class members
  names of all girls in the class
  names of all boys in the class
  vocabulary words
  spelling words
  homonyms
  antonyms
  synonyms
  categories such as fruits, vegetables, etc.
- Let the class make word search puzzles for others to work.
- Make a math problem search.
- Help the substitute teacher by putting a student's name on each line to keep track of the work handed in for the day.

MATH | ANTONYMS | HOMONYMS | SYNONYMS | SPELLING

GRID

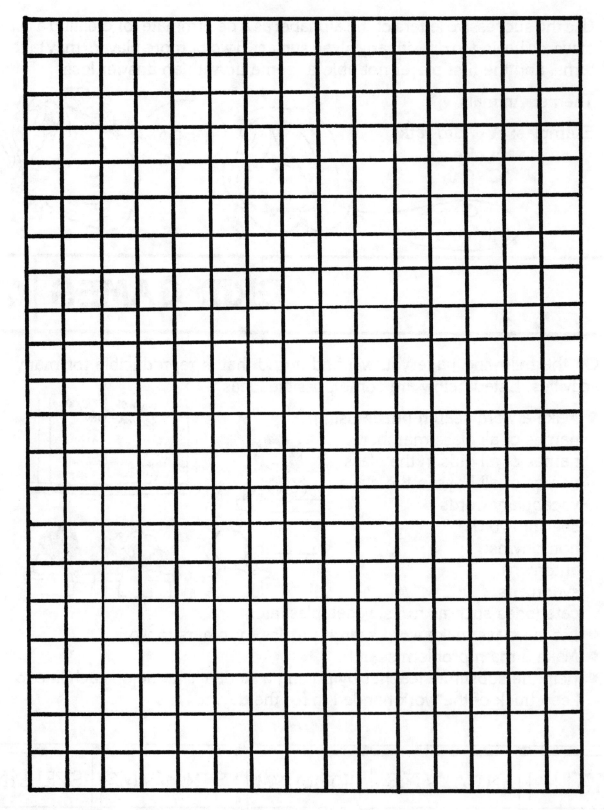

Have you ever tried to float an egg? If you have, you have observed that as it hits the water it sinks and rests on the bottom. Try this experiment and see what happens to your sinking egg!

Fill a drinking glass with fresh water. Put an egg in the water and watch it sink to the bottom of the glass. Now, slowly pour two or more tablespoons of table salt into the water. If some of the undissolved salt collects on the top of the egg, use a spoon and turn the egg over. As soon as the salt dissolves, observe what happens to the egg! Also, observe the changes in the appearance of the water!

What happened and why? As you know, the egg is heavier than the water, so it sinks. But salt is very heavy and when it dissolves in water, it causes the water to become heavier. When this happens the egg eventually rises because it is lighter than the water around it.

You cannot see salt when it dissolves but table salt is not pure salt. Table salt has been crystalized around a minute piece of starch. Since starch does not dissolve, the water becomes milky or cloudy. Look to see if you can see the tiny pieces of starch in the water!

Listed below are the names of the male, female and their young in different animal families. Read the three names of each family and have the class identify the family name.

MALE	FEMALE	YOUNG	(FAMILY)
1. Buck	Doe	Bunny	(Rabbit)
2. Gander	Goose	Gosling	(Goose)
3. Buck	Doe	Fawn	(Deer)
4. Lion	Lioness	Cub	(Lion)
5. Sire	Bitch	Puppy	(Dog)
6. Jack	Jenny	Foal	(Jackass)
7. Drake	Duck	Duckling	(Duck)
8. Tom	Queen	Kitten	(Cat)
9. Stallion	Mare	Foal	(Horse)
10. Ram	Ewe	Lamb	(Sheep)
11. Bull	Cow	Calf	(Whale)
12. Boar	Sow	Piglet	(Swine)

BEND A BONE! | 73

Here is a fun, interesting experiment that turns a bone into rubber! Place a chicken leg or wishbone into a glass of vinegar. It will take a wishbone about three days to soften and a leg bone about a week. The vinegar dissolves the calcium in the bone and the bone becomes rubbery, bending easily.

ANYONE FOR A RUBBERY EGG? | 74

Place a raw egg in a small glass or bowl filled with enough vinegar to cover the egg. Leave the egg in the vinegar for a day or two. Vinegar is an acid which will dissolve the calcium in the eggshell, leaving only a thin, rubbery skin around the egg.

You can fool your friends with the rubbery egg, because they won't be able to tell by looking which egg is rubbery in a carton of normal eggs. Be careful, though. The inside of the egg is runny and if it is squeezed too hard it will break!

If you have been studying about trees in Science class, this would be a good exercise to use. If you have not been studying about trees, this could be used on Arbor Day or any day for fun!

Ask the students to name a tree that reminds them of the phrases below:

Example: The remains of something that has burned.   (Ash)

1. A person that is old   (Elder)
2. Something that stretches   (Rubber)
3. A bright color   (Orange)
4. A nut   (Walnut)
5. Small insect   (Locust)
6. Another name for cleaning up   (Spruce)
7. OK spelled with an "a" inside   (Oak)
8. A present for the teacher   (Apple)
9. The most "knotty" wood   (Pine)

To perform this experiment, you will need a small piece of paper, a match, a glass and a saucer which has been filled with water.

Light the paper and place it in the glass while the paper is burning. Then turn the glass over and put it in the saucer which has been filled with water. To everyone's amazement, the water will rise into the glass until the last drop is gone from the saucer!

MAKE YOUR OWN FOG! | 77

You will need an empty, dry, clean, tall jar, a glass of hot water (boiling if possible) and several ice cubes stuck together. Now pour the water into the bottle. Set the ice cubes on top of the bottle and arrange them so that as little air as possible can get past them into the bottle. Next, hold the bottle up to the light. What you see swirling in the bottle is fog! The hot water warmed the air directly above it in the bottle and this warm air rose. The cool air under the ice formed tiny drops of water and this made the air in the bottle damp and cloudy. This combination of warm and cool air makes fog.

78 | THROUGH THE READING GLASS

For this experiment you will need a stiff piece of paper, a pin and a book. Make a tiny pinhole in the paper and you will have a reading glass. Now, cover one eye with your hand, hold the paper up to the other eye and look through the pinhole at a page in the book. The print looks sharper to you now than when you look at it with both eyes. Why? Because your eye is being forced to focus through this tiny hole in the stiff paper and has to concentrate on a single object.

79 | MAKE YOUR OWN MAGNIFYING GLASS!

For this experiment you will need a piece of waxed paper, some water, an eyedropper and a book. Place the waxed paper over a page in the book and try to read through it. The letters under the waxed paper will be difficult to see because they will be blurred. With the eye-dropper put a small drop of water on the waxed paper. Now, try reading through the water. The letters that you see through the water will seem clearer and larger than before. The reason is because the rounded top of the water-drop forms a lens similar to the lens in a microscope. Scientist Anthony Van Leeuwenhoek found that glass curved upward toward the eye would magnify or make things look bigger. Therefore the drop of water acts like a microscope.

EARTHWORMS - You will find the longest earthworms living in Australia. They can be as long as 12 feet from end to end. Their bodies are thick and look somewhat like a garden hose.

SNAKES - Did you know that snakes are totally deaf? So, the pictures that you have seen of a snake charmer and a snake are deceiving. The snake is not charmed by the music but by the movements of the charmer as he sways back and forth.

TORTOISES - Few animals live longer than humans. The tortoise's life is probably the longest of the animals. A male tortoise has been reported to have lived over 152 years!

MAKE A CRYSTAL GARDEN! | 81

To make a crystal garden you will need 1 Tablespoon ammonia, ¼ cup water and ¼ cup salt. Put a piece of coal in a pie tin and cover it with the mixture above. Then add food coloring on the top. Watch it grow!

Give each student a piece of white construction paper (8½ x 11) and have them draw a picture on one side. Depending on the grade level, have the students turn their pictures over and draw a specific number of lines on the back to form a puzzle. (for example, if you have a first grade class have them draw 4 lines to make 5 puzzle pieces out of their picture - the older students may make more pieces to their puzzles) Then have each student cut on the lines, turn the pieces over and put their own puzzle together. Then have them mix the pieces of their puzzle on their desk, find a partner and work each other's puzzle. After a given time, have the students change partners and repeat the process.

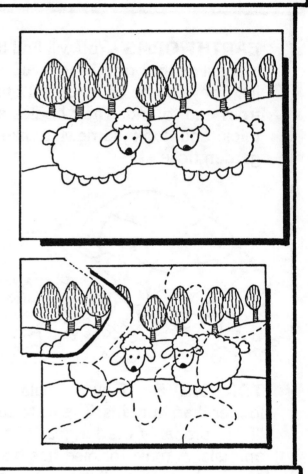

For added dimension the nose can be a separate piece of paper. Fold the nose & glue it onto the face.

This art activity adds lots of atmosphere to the classroom at Halloween, because it is fun, easy, and everyone enjoys his end product. Give each student a piece of white construction paper (8½ x 11), a piece of black construction paper (approx. 5 x 8) and 8 - 10 strips of newspaper (approx. 1" wide by 14" long). Instruct the students to make a witch's face on the white paper with their crayons (the uglier the better). Then have them curl the strips of newspaper with their pencils and glue the strips on the face.

Create a harvest festival atmosphere in the classroom for November by making scarecrows using a white piece of construction paper (8½ x 11) and a paper towel. To make the head of the scarecrow, wad up the paper towel, place it on the paper and trace lightly around it. Then draw the scarecrow using crayons. Encourage the students to make their illustration over the entire sheet of paper. After they have finished coloring, glue the scarecrow's head in the proper place and pin the project up on the bulletin board.

Using brown paper bags that you can secure at a local supermarket (use the size larger than the lunch bag size) and crayons, the students can make reindeer masks for themselves, or if the class is older they can make them to take to the kindergarten class. Cut six inches off of the bottom of the bag and use this portion for the antlers. Make the antlers by having the students trace around their hands.

86 | JANUARY Funny paper snowman

For a unique looking snowman try using the comic strips! All that is needed to make this snowman is an 8½ x 11 sheet of white construction paper, some comic strips and crayons. The two or three body parts can be cut circularly or for added interest they can be cut in snowflake fashion. After the body has been cut, glue it onto the white construction paper. Make special features with crayons.

87 | February Make a Valentine Snowflake

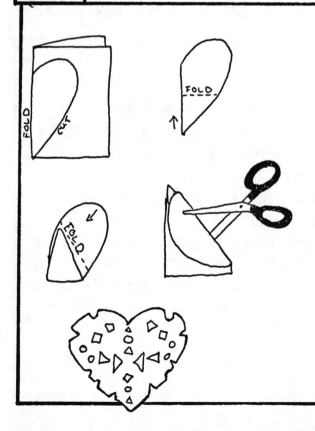

For something different to do when making valentines try this idea! All you need is a red piece of construction paper for each student. Fold the paper only once as if you were going to make a snowflake. The first cut that you make must be in the shape of a valentine. After the valentine shape is cut, fold the valentine to make the inside cuts like those on a snowflake. When all of the cutting has been completed open the snowflake to find that you have a red valentine snowflake. Hang it on the bulletin board just the way it is or glue onto white construction paper first before hanging.

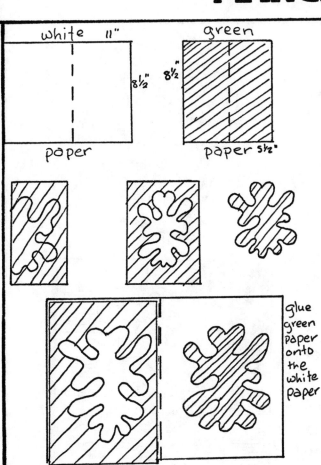

To help decorate the room for the month of March try this fun project that intrigues all ages. Give each student one white sheet of construction paper (8½ x 11) and one sheet of green construction paper (8½ x 5½). Have the students fold both sheets of paper in half. (see folding directions) Using the green sheet, cut out shapes, designs, etc. on the fold. Save both the cutouts and the paper from which they were cut. Now glue these shapes on half of the white sheet and glue the paper from which they were cut on the other half of the white sheet. The older the students, the more sophisticated the design or shapes. This is one very effective way to decorate for St. Patrick's Day.

APRIL Spring cards | 89

For something different take a stamp pad or tempera paint to school (tempera takes longer to dry). Give each student a piece of white construction paper approximately 4" x 11". Fold the white paper in half (see folding directions). On the front half of the folded sheet have the students make 5 fingerprints using the stamp pad or paint. Then have them make the details of the little chicks with their crayons. On the inside of the card write "Happy Spring."

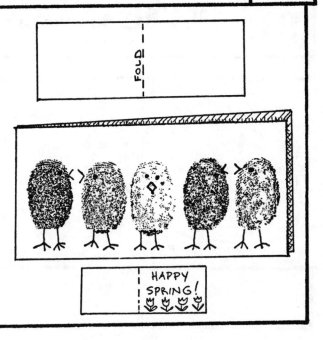

Try this idea for something different and fun. Cut out pictures of interesting objects from old magazines. Use pictures with lots of detail for older children and less detail for younger children.

Provide each student with an 8½ x 11 sheet of white construction paper and instruct them to pick out one of the pictures you have cut out. Ask the students to fold the paper in half and then cut the object from the magazine in half.

Next, ask them to glue one half of the magazine picture on the fold line and with their pencils draw the other half of the object on the other side of the paper.

Encourage them to make their drawings fun and interesting. Have some extra magazines on hand for those students who get inspired and want to do a second picture!

This nit-wit swims alone in a thunderstorm.

This super-wit swims on a nice day with a buddy where there is a lifeguard.

Discuss summer safety and then give the students a white piece of construction paper (12" x 18") and have them fold it in half. On one half of the paper have the students draw a "nit wit" who is not practicing summer safety. Then on the other half of the paper have them draw a "super wit" who is practicing summer safety. If time permits have them write a sentence under each illustration and share their illustrations with the class.

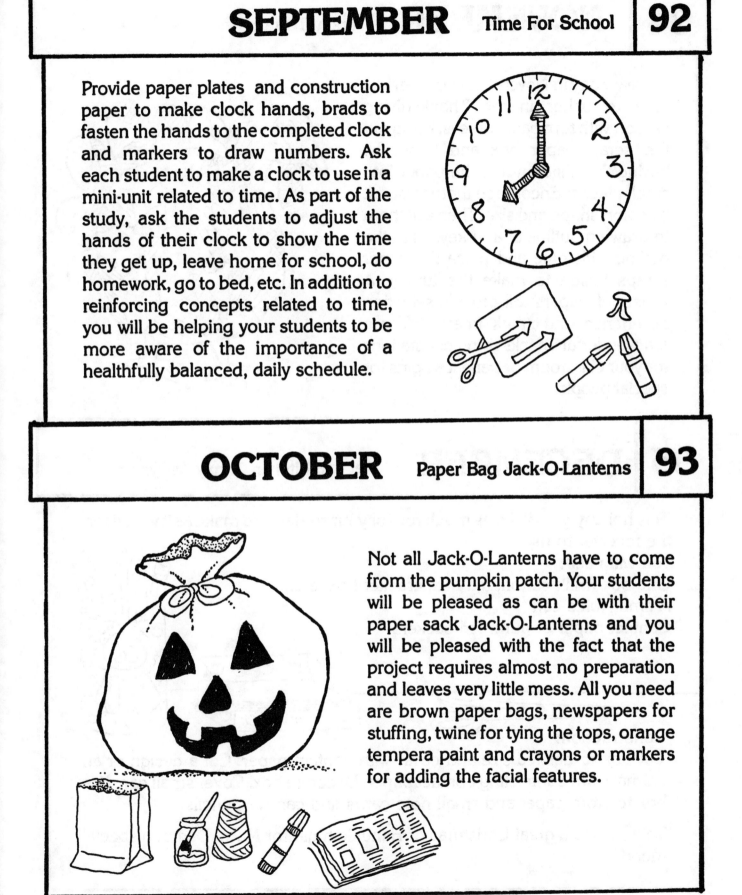

SEPTEMBER — Time For School — 92

Provide paper plates and construction paper to make clock hands, brads to fasten the hands to the completed clock and markers to draw numbers. Ask each student to make a clock to use in a mini-unit related to time. As part of the study, ask the students to adjust the hands of their clock to show the time they get up, leave home for school, do homework, go to bed, etc. In addition to reinforcing concepts related to time, you will be helping your students to be more aware of the importance of a healthfully balanced, daily schedule.

OCTOBER — Paper Bag Jack-O-Lanterns — 93

Not all Jack-O-Lanterns have to come from the pumpkin patch. Your students will be pleased as can be with their paper sack Jack-O-Lanterns and you will be pleased with the fact that the project requires almost no preparation and leaves very little mess. All you need are brown paper bags, newspapers for stuffing, twine for tying the tops, orange tempera paint and crayons or markers for adding the facial features.

94 | NOVEMBER   Turkey Tear-Ups

A dreary day in November is the perfect time to usher in the Thanksgiving season with torn page turkeys. Bring out the scrap paper box and begin by having the children tear the paper into small pieces. Encourage them to sort it by color, shape and size. Then ask them to draw an outline of a turkey, fill in the outline with glue and place the paper scraps inside to make the turkey. A variety of papers will provide selection experience and spark interest. These are wonderful Thanksgiving decorations for your classroom or perfect as gifts for special people.

95 | DECEMBER   Recycle Kitchen Throw Aways

This holiday gift will be as much fun for your students to make as it will be for the receiver to use.

You will need:
One box (milk carton, tea box, cracker box, etc.)
A small juice can
Contact paper or gummed stickers

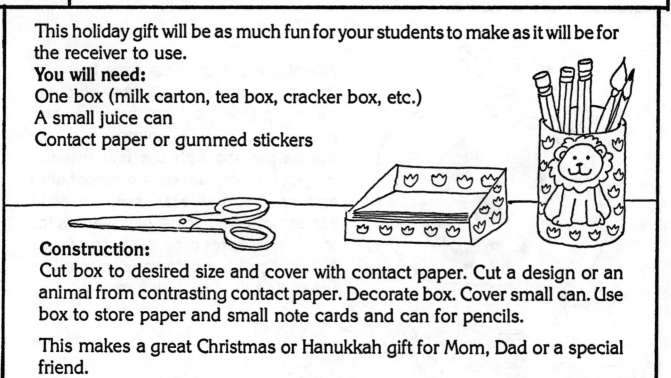

Construction:
Cut box to desired size and cover with contact paper. Cut a design or an animal from contrasting contact paper. Decorate box. Cover small can. Use box to store paper and small note cards and can for pencils.

This makes a great Christmas or Hanukkah gift for Mom, Dad or a special friend.

January is the perfect time to study the calendar! Provide each student with a copy of a January calendar page. Ask each student to fill in the numbers and days of the week, family birthdays, school events and any other special days. Then lead a class discussion on the history of the calendar. You may want to do a little research yourself so that you have a few interesting tid-bits to share. For starters you could use these facts:

- The calendar we use got its start in ancient Egypt.

- The word calendar came from the Roman word calends, which was the first day of every month.

- Ancient men kept track of time according to the moon, which is the reason our calendar is divided into moons, or months.

Provide large sheets of construction paper and art supplies. Have the students draw a large heart and write the name of a very special person in the middle of the heart. Then instruct them to fill the heart with words, slogans, phrases, pictures and symbols to express their feelings for the person. Cutting the hearts out and delivering them to the lucky person will be a bonus activity. This could also be a good way to express appreciation to people who work in the school such as the principal, custodian, secretary, cafeteria workers or school nurse.

St. Patrick's day is the perfect time to celebrate the color green. Plan for everyone (the teacher, too) to wear as much green as possible. Ask the cafeteria to cooperate by preparing a green lunch. If this is impossible, improvise by furnishing green Kool-Aid, green frosted cookies, celery sticks or zucchini chunks for an afternoon treat.

Provide green construction paper for making shamrocks to be worn all day. Lots of green markers and crayons for an art project will add to the festivities, too. A word search puzzle with 10 to 20 hidden words that represent green things will help soothe your conscience by adding some language practice to the "green day" schedule. And of course, you will want to select a very special story about the jolly little leprechauns to bring a touch of Irish folklore into your classroom.

99 | **APRIL**   Pussy Willow Pictures

Bring spring into your classroom with Pussy Willow Pictures. Provide construction paper, glue, crayons or markers and a bowl of puffed wheat or oat cereal. Instruct the students to draw branches with a marker or crayon and glue the cereal on the branches to give a pussy willow effect. True, some cereal will most likely make its way from hand to mouth rather than from hand to paper, but after all, it is nutritious. The finished creations will make an attractive bulletin board display or booklet covers.

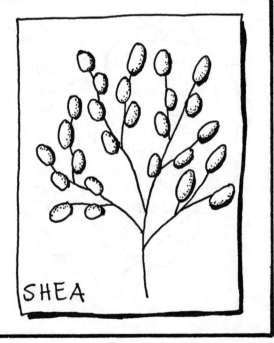

SHEA

For a challenging, instant art activity that is sure to result in lively conversation, ask students to use drawing paper and markers to draw hidden picture designs. Use a seasonal theme such as spring flowers, birds, trees or insects and specify the number to be hidden in each design. (example, 5 spring flowers, etc.) Allow only 5 or ten minutes for the designs to be finished. Then ask students to exchange completed designs and find the hidden pictures.

Have your students make frames for their own photographs. Use cardboard, yarn, glue, pictures, and scissors.

Cut two cardboard shapes slightly larger than the photograph. Cut out the center of one piece, leaving 3/4" border. Wrap yarn around the border, very closely. Glue the loose ends to the back. Glue the photograph to the second piece of cardboard. Now glue photograph to the yarn frame. If you need a stand, use a firm piece of cardboard glued to the back outside of the frame. Decorate with buttons, ribbons, yarn, etc.

These fancy framed photographs are sure to make a hit with Mom or Dad on their special day.